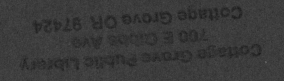
917.04

WHERE THE WEST BEGINS

America's

Plains & Prairies

Text and Photography by

KAREN KENT

DEDICATION

To my mother Dorothy for the privilege of being her daughter.

ACKNOWLEDGMENTS

There are many people who have helped bring this book to fruition. First of all, I would like to thank Deborah Hastings, vice-president/publisher at SMITHMARK, for making the book possible. Sandra Still, my editor, has been involved and nurtured this book from its very beginning over four years ago.

Agfa Corporation has been exceedingly generous in providing film for this project. One of the many contributions of Dominick Proprieti, president of K & L Tarturo Imaging in New York, was to develop hundreds of rolls of film. My friend Paul Land, of RC Communicaitons in Manhattan, who assists my career in many ways, printed the traveling photography exhibition that accompanies the book.

I received invaluable assistance from all the states' visitors and tourism bureaus on a statewide level, as well as assistance from local city tourism offices. These people really helped make the content of the book possible. A particular thank you to Dawn Charging of North Dakota, and to all the people I met, stayed with, interviewed, and photographed in the Plains and Prairies.

An appreciative acknowledgment goes to my partner San Rabin, for his commitment and support in all aspects of this book, including teaching me to navigate in the computer world and giving me a Mac powerbook on which I authored the text.

I am grateful to my parents Norman and Dorothy Blass, and my children April Shultz and Alan Kent, for their love, encouragement, and inspiration. Recognition also to Doug Sheer for all his efforts during my early years in New York. And to my friend, Joe Lanciotti, for so much.

A special thank you to John Puffer who opened the door to photography for me more than twenty-five years ago.

This edition published by SMITHMARK Publishers Inc.,
16 East 32nd Street, New York, NY 10016

SMITHMARK books are available for bulk purchase for sales promotion and premium use.
For details write or call the manager of special sales, 16 East 32nd Street, New York, NY 10016; (212) 532-6600.

This book was designed and produced by
Todtri Productions Limited
P.O. Box 20058
New York, NY 10023-1482
Fax: (212) 279-1241

Printed and bound in Singapore

Library of Congress Catalog Card Number 95-067562

ISBN 0-8317-8172-6

All photographs by Karen Kent © 1995

Author: Karen Kent

Producer: Robert M. Tod
Book Designer: Mark Weinberg
Production Coordinator: Heather Weigel
Photo Editor: Edward Douglas
Editors: Sandra Still, Don Kennison
Typesetting: Command-O, NYC

CONTENTS

Above:
A young deer
listens for intruders
in the prairie
grasses of North
Dakota's Badlands.

Left:
Under a winter sky and
a setting sun, the prairies
of South Dakota's
Badlands are a place
of exquisite solitude.

PROLOGUE

Clocks don't work on the prairies. There is a stillness, a silence within, that has something to do with time as well as solitude. In this space perhaps one can hear for the first time. Clarity is evoked, revealing an inner harmony. Everything is clear. Songs of bobolinks and meadowlarks. Your own footsteps. Rustle of aspen leaves. Prairie cordgrass billowing in the wind. You see more clearly. Tracks of a mule deer. A badger hole in the thicket. A cicada under a stone. Chokecherry in bloom. An open horizon of earth and sky.

You take your place in the environment—just another creature, connected to all other creatures—and in this timeless moment you have some small awareness of how it all works, how it's all just so.

Introduction

Prairie Tales

I grew up on a farm in northwest Iowa some forty years ago. One of my greatest joys was riding my Arabian pony, Gypsy, as close to Indian style as I could. Bareback, sometimes bridleless, I galloped over pastures and streams. I would crouch along her neck and ride under low-hanging branches, emulating the Indians. After a while I was able to pass this test without being brushed off. I imagined discovering the lakes, streams, and prairie hunting grounds for the first time, like the Ioways before me.

Our farm had plenty of pasture and many untilled acres around barns and sheds, with giant cottonwoods my brothers and I could climb, pretending to be Indian scouts. We searched near the bluffs and creeks for arrowheads and other artifacts we could use to tell the story of the Great Plains Indians. A few miles from our farm was the site of the Spirit Lake Massacre, where Abigail Sharp, a young girl at the time, survived an Indian raid as a captive after her family was killed and their cabin burned. She was later dramatically rescued and spent the rest of her life retelling her story to an eager public.

Some farms were like the one next to ours, where every available inch of land was cultivated. There were no trees or yards to play in, just rows of tilled soil filled with stalks of corn growing in the summer. In the winter, row after row of white-covered stubble surrounded a desolate, unpainted gray house. There had been groves of old cottonwoods but they had been cut away to produce more rows of corn. Eventually the farmer left, his house was torn down, and that scrap of land, too, was plowed and planted.

Following page:
Gold and rust-colored fall grasses grace the Konza Prairie Preserve in Kansas, the largest tall-grass prairie in the country.

Right:
Seven-year-old Andrea Hanson rides her horse through a field of blooming clover near Bowman, North Dakota.

Left:
Mike Shultz, a present-day farrier, shoes a horse. Farriers, otherwise known as blacksmiths, carry on the traditions of a vanishing craft.

I used to ride my horse for miles—to Lake Okoboji, Spirit Lake, Swan Lake, and all points in between. I rode her to Superior, a town of two hundred people, where I went to grade school. It was a generic small Iowa town: a church, two general stores, a bar, a cafe, a gas station and garage, a post office, a co-operative grain elevator, and the town telephone operator, who ran the switchboard from her home.

One summer day, some older boys thought it would be great fun if I rode Gypsy into the town bar. Just like a western movie, I thought, as my horse and I passed into a darkly lit space with old wooden chairs, planked wood floors, a pool table, and several men in their dusty work clothes and bandannas, standing at the bar. I had never been in a bar before, and I didn't know what to expect. The daytime darkness smelled exotic. The bartender yelled at me to get that horse out—now! Gypsy, perhaps looking for something to drink, knocked over a few glasses of beer. We left ignominiously, my face flushed and prickly, no longer playing a scene from *How the West Was Won*, followed out the door by unrelenting laughter from the boys who had dared me to enter. We galloped into the bright sunlight, turned along the railroad tracks, and headed home. I didn't come back for more.

On Friday nights in Superior, people would come to town, park at the foot of the unpaved main street where the railroad tracks and grain elevators met, bring lawn chairs and popcorn, buy sodas from the general stores, and watch free movies projected on the side of a low, white cement building. I had my first passionate, illicit teenage kiss watching *Creature from the Black Lagoon*. This kiss had the same elements of danger, the same lure of doing something taboo and feeling exotic in this wholesome farmland as did my ride into the bar.

My old two-story, brick schoolhouse has since been torn down, and most of the stores have closed; only the cafe remains. The grain elevators prospered. Now giant cement monoliths inhabit the town, surrounding a small, white, wooden Methodist church and towering over acres and acres of fertile prairie farmland.

Below:
The late-day sun highlights a quintessential main street in a small plains town in Iowa.

Prairie Roots

It was exhilarating to ride over the rolling grassy plains on my horse, feeling the sting of wind, the heat of prairie sun, and the openness of land, as open as the sea that let my imagination stretch over time to eons before me to the Cambrian Period, 570 million years ago, when the prairie I loved was a vast sea. Now sharks' teeth, coral reefs, and other fossils remain trapped in bedrock along cliffs, riverbanks, and valleys of the Missouri, Mississippi, and Des Moines rivers.

Where the great glaciers trailed some 2.5 million years ago, during the Cenozoic Era, they left deposits that became mountains, plateaus, buttes, mesas, sandhills, escarpments, riverbeds, and rich prairie sod. Only 150 years ago, pioneers from the eastern states and immigrants from Europe broke the prairie's cover and plowed under most of the 600 million acres of native grasslands that covered the entire mid-continent.

Prairie grasses once grew as high as eight feet. Native grasses include big and little bluestem, blue gramma, needle grass, silver beardgrass, buffalo grass, threadleaf sedge, and slender wheat grass. The grasses undulated with wild flowers: morning glory, sunflower, prairie rose, phlox, milkweed, goldenrod, curlycup gumweed, and scarlet globe mallow.

Many creatures made their homes on the prairies. A host of thriving insects lived alongside such diverse grazing animals as bison, pronghorn deer, elk, jackrabbit, and prairie dog. Only vestiges of some of these species remain today in the overcultivated, overfertilized lands. There are just a few thousand acres of natural prairies left to remind us of the magnificent sea of grass that once deceived explorers into believing this was a vast desert region, devoid of minerals and trees, and therefore worthless and totally uninhabitable.

Above:
A golden spike commemorating the completion of the first transcontinental railroad sits in Council Bluffs, Iowa, site of its eastern terminus.

Explorers

By the early 1700s trade was an important activity for Indians and Europeans. In 1673 the French explorers Louis Jolliet and Father Marquette traveled down the Mississippi River as far as what is now St. Louis and then headed back to Montreal. Next to arrive was another Frenchman, Sieur de la Salle, who laid claim to the Mississippi Valley for Louis XIV, and called it Louisiana. Fur traders, primarily French, continued trading and moving across the plains and made it into the Rockies by 1750.

The Americans Meriwether Lewis and William Clark, journeying across the plains via the Missouri River, set out to explore a path to the Pacific in 1803, just as France sold the entire Louisiana Territory, some 800,000 square miles, to the United States for only 15 million dollars.

This journey by Lewis and Clark marked President Thomas Jefferson's third attempt to send an expedition into the western areas of the country. After Lewis and Clark returned from the Pacific, Zebulon Pike crossed the plains to get to the Rockies in 1806. Stephen Long led a third official expedition in 1819 to protect the fur trade and deter the British by setting up forts. All three expeditions characterized the Great Plains as desert land, uninhabitable and undesirable, lacking trees, water, and minerals. It became known as the Great American Desert on the maps and in the minds of the rest of the country.

Left:
The county
courthouse of
Dubuque, Iowa,
is a Romanesque
structure built in
1893 from Indiana
limestone and brick.

Left:
This is one of many
eclectic houses built
in Atchison, Kansas,
during the late nine-
teenth century, when
the prosperous town
was a major outfit-
ting center for wagon
trains headed west.

Right:
In 1881 a thirty-one-
room mansion was
constructed in Inde-
pendence, Missouri,
for Harvey Vaile,
a wealthy builder
of the Erie Canal.
The Vaile Mansion
is now a museum,
a piece of history
of the early West.

Plains Indians

Blackfoot Indians were one of the oldest indigenous tribes in the northernmost part of the plains, living in the Mackenzie River area over two thousand years ago. By 1775 most of the tribal migrations into the Great Plains had ended, and their boundaries were set. A nomadic plains Indian culture then came into being and flourished until about 1875. It was based on buffalo hunting and aided by the horse, which had been brought in by Spanish explorers.

Thirty-one Indian nations existed on the plains: to the north were the Blackfoot, Cree, Assiniboine, Gros Ventre, Crow, Hidatsa, Mandan, Arikara, and Sarsi; in the central plains were the Sioux, Cheyenne, Arapaho, Ponca, Pawnee, Oto, Omaha, Iowa, Missouri, Sauk, and Fox; to the south were the Kansa, Osage, Kiowa, Comanche, Kiowa Apache, Wichita, Jicarilla Apache, and Lipan Apache; in the Rockies were the Shoshone, Ute, Nez Perce, and the Flatheads. Their entire population probably was no more than two hundred thousand. The Blackfoot, with thirty thousand people; the Sioux, with twenty-seven thousand; the Pawnee, with twenty thousand; and the Comanche and Assiniboine with ten thousand each, were the largest and most dominant tribes.

These great nations of the American plains became known as horse warriors. Most tribes had little to do with each other, however, and they never banded together as one to try and repel the white men, with the exception of the defeat of General Custer at Little Big Horn in 1876. But by then it was too late.

They engaged in many skirmishes against each other, but never in all out warfare. Their battles were part of a way of life for them; they raided one another to steal horses, to get revenge, or to protect their tribe. Their lives revolved around the Great Spirit, which was manifest in the creatures of the land, especially the buffalo.

Everything the Indians did was an aspect of religious ritual; from the circular construction of the tipi, with its opening facing east for morning prayer, to the buffalo hunt and the war party.

The bison, a creature that had been on the plains for two million years, numbering at least seventy million, eventually became a target for white buffalo hunters when a tanning process that made fine leather from buffalo hides was implemented in 1860.

The plains Indians were trained to be warriors and hunters from the time of birth. Boys were taught to endure many hardships that would toughen them. They were constantly being tested for cowardice; if a boy failed, he wasn't allowed to be a warrior. For this insufficiency he had to live with the women and be one of them, even in dress.

As adolescents, the young men proved their readiness by scalping an enemy or stealing his horse. As grown men, their entire life was given over to the tribe. Their social life was filled with song and dance; nearly every occasion of their daily routines such as harvesting, hunting, mourning, war, and religion was accompanied by ritual dancing.

What the so-called civilized world saw as barbaric was instead the result of living with nature, reacting as nature does, which is often harsh and unforgiving.

Above:
A young participant in the colorful Mesquakie Indian Powwow at Tama, Iowa, gets ready for his performance.

Left:
Keith Bear, a member of the Three Affiliated Tribes of North Dakota, plays his handmade flute at the Knife River Indian Cultural Celebration.

Above:
Fifteen hundred
bison roam free in the
73,000-acre Custer
State Park in South
Dakota. The park,
opened in 1919, is
now the second-
largest state park in
the United States and
has one of the largest
public buffalo herds
in the country.

In the late nineteenth century the Indians were herded from state to state, to reservation after reservation, where they died of starvation and disease, as the white men took more and more Indian land for their own uses. By 1876, both Indian and buffalo were nearly wiped out. The seventy million bison were reduced in number to only a thousand in less than a thirty-year period.

The last gasp of Indian life was extinguished by the massacre of several hundred Sioux Indians at Wounded Knee, South Dakota, in 1890. A way of life that seemed immortal was wiped out, and the great golden age of the mystic plains warriors had ended.

Populism in the Prairies

There is still something wild and free in the prairies, even though the land has been turned into farms and more farms followed by ranches. The air is intoxicating in its purity and the skies are free of pollution; there are yet vast stretches of sparsely populated land open to the horizon. It's easy to feel unencumbered by laws and regulations required for large groups of urban people; in the plains, living with a few neighbors, one's wits and common sense seem to be enough.

It is, of course, an illusion of freedom. There have always been forces at work here against that freedom since the white man began living out his code of manifest destiny, and laws have on the whole favored corporations. In the 1800s the railroads and the banks garnered special treatment. The farmers, encouraged by the railroads with promises of a good life, bought land from the railroads. The land they bought was land in the public domain that had been given to the railroads by government grants.

After the Civil War, the U.S. government deflated the value of currency by giving banks an advantage at the expense of farmers and other debtors. The farmers finally rebelled against these economic policies and legislations. In the 1870s farmers formed a number of alliances, such as the Grange and the Greenbacks. They joined with the Populist Movement in the 1890s, which was headed by the outspoken lawyer and politician William Jennings Bryan, who was the Populist candidate for president in 1896 and 1900. Bryan was fighting against the gold standard. He preferred a silver standard that would help the beleaguered farmers with easier financing. Bryan never won the presidency, but many reforms that the Populists stood for did in fact become law.

L. Frank Baum, author of many children's books including the classic Oz series, set in Kansas, was also a populist supporter. A political interpretation of *The Wizard of Oz* as a populist allegory relates that Oz, (the abbreviation for ounce, the unit used to measure gold) symbolized the use of the gold standard. Further, the Cowardly Lion represented Bryan, whom Baum supported without much enthusiasm; Tin Man stood for people without jobs, discarded by factories in their embrace of the Industrial Revolution; Scarecrow represented the farmer who didn't have the brains or organization to take on the government. The Wicked Witch of the East was the nefarious banker exploiting the little people. In the book Dorothy was wearing silver slippers, symbolizing Baum's desire for the silver standard. She traveled down the Yellow Road, which was the gold standard. The Wizard, of course, was the president of the United States, isolated in

Below:
Ocher-colored prairie grasses shine in the fall sunlight near Castle Rock, Kansas.

Washington in the White House (Emerald City), creating an image that appeared to be just what the people wanted. Dorothy's fellow travelers unmasked him as a charlatan and an antipopulist.

The larger issues of fairness and freedom were never resolved in favor of the people, since lawmakers and capitalists were in control then, and still are today. The social environment created as a context for daily life is seldom examined, and people function within it as best they can, left with an illusion of freedom that seems real if it's not examined too closely. In the empty, wide, open space where the tallest structures are grain elevators dotting the prairie plains, a person can inhabit one's own personal universe without being infringed on by others.

Cowboys on the Plains

Farmers and ranchers, while natural antagonists, had in common the pioneering traits of adapting to the land and working hard to make a living from it. They had differing uses for the plains; the farmers kept expanding their settlements, going farther into the western plains, into arid cattle country. They were assisted in their quest to fence and plow the land after barbed wire was invented and when windmills, with heads that pivoted in the direction of the wind, were mass produced.

Westerners' need for laws was entirely different from those of easterners, who legislated for the entire country. Many laws, based on the common laws of England, were useful in the East but had little practicality in the newly settled West, which had to adopt a new set of rules for survival

Below:
Bucked off by his bronco, a rodeo rider bites the dust in Sidney, Iowa.

Above:
In a moment of final
preparation, a cowboy
gets ready to leave the
chute in the Brahma
bull-riding event at the
Sidney, Iowa, rodeo.

in an unknown environment. Laws governing land grants were based on how many acres a farmer needed and could cultivate in the forested lands of the East. Usually, forty acres was plenty for one man and his mule to farm. Western farmers had the capability to cultivate larger acreages, and needed to do so for survival. The same was true for ranchers, who needed ranges in the thousands of acres to make a living.

Life on the plains demanded different ways of being, and the cowboy was the first American to adapt to his new surroundings in a natural way. The reign of the cattle kingdom was brief but dramatic, and it lives on in western mythology. The days of the great cattle trails on which cowboys drove their herds, mostly Texas longhorns, to markets in Santa Fe, New Mexico, Wichita, Kansas, and other railroad depots lasted approximately forty-five years, from 1840 to 1885. The cowboy had to become proficient in riding a horse to tend his cattle. His enemies on the plains, the Indians, were extremely skilled and dangerous horsemen. The old weapons of the East, the single-shot rifle and pistols, were virtually useless against the Indian.

It wasn't until Samuel Colt invented the six-shooter in 1838 that the white man held an advantage over the Indian. The Texas Rangers were the first to use the new weapon, with telling results. Unfortunately, there weren't enough customers, and Colt went bankrupt in 1842, waiting for the government to recognize the six-shooter's importance. It finally did so during the U. S.-Mexican War of 1846-48, and placed an order so large that, because Colt had no facilities of his own, he had to farm out to manufacture them all. Sam Colt became a millionaire within a few years.

Above:
The interior lobby of Union Station in St. Louis—called
the Grand Hall—is a majestic space filled with mosaics,
gold leaf, and stained glass. At the time it was built
in 1894, it was the largest railroad station in the world.

Left:
At the conclusion
of the day's dances
in Tama, Iowa, the
American flag is
lowered in a solemn
ceremony during
the annual Mesquakie
Indian Powwow.

Right:
In the dead of winter, horses depend on hay brought in to them at the Wild Horse Sanctuary in Hot Springs, South Dakota.

Below:
A brief, but intense, storm darkens the sky with rain even as a rainbow arches over an Iowan cornfield.

Left:
Russet-colored
grasses and bales
of hay behind fences
are softly muted
under winter's light
near the Black Hills
in South Dakota.

Weather

There are many things that seem to happen on a grand scale in the plains and prairies. So much reaches mythic proportions that reality gets blurred in romantic visions of prairie life, as in the blissful movie *Field of Dreams*, which equates being in Iowa with being in heaven.

But what is real is the weather. And almost everyone's livelihood depends on weather. What is most destructive to life is lack of water—a drought. Dreaded since settlers began arriving in the plains in the early 1800s, droughts still can ruin lives. By definition, plains have arid or semiarid climates, receiving fifteen to twenty-five inches of rainfall annually.

Prairie winds blow constantly and at velocities found only at the seashore. Winter blizzards of snow and wind, and chinooks blowing up to one hundred miles per hour in the northern plains, blanket the terrain in snow drifts and bring human endeavors to a standstill. Hot, dry summer winds sear and blister crops and carry dirt and topsoil for thousands of miles. Tornadoes, awesome and twisting funnels that are land-bound hurricanes, last only minutes but uproot trees, flatten barns and houses, carry off livestock, and generally wreak havoc, testifying to the terrifying power of wind.

Winds are pervasive on the prairies; their force shows in the faces of the people, where sharply etched lines give evidence of its passing. There is nothing to slow down the relentless velocity of the wind. There are no barriers, no windbreakers. Cool, refreshing breezes that are gentle to the spirit do exist as well; but whatever gives pleasure in this land often brings pain in another, more intense, form.

The dust bowls of the mid-1930s were the fiercest example of dust storms, which have always occurred on prairies. In the 1930s the plains experienced a drought cycle that lasted several years, in which land, overgrazed and overtilled, rose from fields and traveled in hot tornadolike black clouds over the plains to cities like Chicago, burying its buildings with twelve million tons of topsoil; it covered the skies in New York City with such density that a virtual blackout occurred for hours. Then it moved on to Boston, and finally out to sea.

If it isn't the lack of rain that's troublesome it's too much precipitation falling as hail or snow, which also wipes out crops and destroys life. Then there is the "freak" snowstorm that falls at the end of April every year, decimating the flowers and wild berries that have just begun to bloom.

Following page:
Rancher Jim Hanson
rides the ranges of
his Logging Camp
Ranch near Bowman,
North Dakota.

Farmers

But people endure. Even though the number of farms and people living on them has shrunk dramatically over the past forty years, people do stay on. And many who left to find employment in small cities or moved to other areas of the country have preferred their lives on the farm, where they could have better shaped their own destinies.

Except that now, there are other forces that also mould one's destiny: land speculators who helped drive up farm prices in the 1970s; banks that encouraged farmers to borrow huge sums at low interest; grain speculators trading on the futures markets at the Board of Trade; government programs to buy and sell grain; and programs to subsidize the farmer.

When the real estate market collapsed in the 1980s, banks called in their loans and foreclosed on many farms. Thousands lost their homes, the farms that had been in their families for generations. Hundreds of small towns were also crippled or eliminated in this same process, since they depended heavily upon the farmer. This resulted not only in the loss of the family farm; it also brought corporate ownership into farming. Today over forty percent of farm owners do not live on their land. In 1950 forty-four percent of all Americans lived on farms and in small towns; today it is closer to twenty-three percent.

Agribusiness is the largest business in the United States today. One billion bushels of wheat are exported yearly, and this feeds one-twelfth of the world's people. There is a price to pay for this seeming bounty. At present, crop lands take out more than they return. Billions of dollars are spent on fertilizer and irrigation. The major underground water supply that runs from the Texas Panhandle through Kansas to South Dakota—the Ogallala Aquifer—is drying up. After being in existence for millions of years, it is being depleted by overproduction and irrigation, and before long the lack of ground water will return the land to its original arid condition, no longer able to produce corn, wheat, milo, and other grains.

These plains, transformed by technology into great crop lands, seem to be going the way of the Indian, the buffalo, and the native grass prairies. Will technology provide a solution for the loss of the aquifer?

Left:
The fall harvest bounty—field corn picked and shelled directly into wagons— is destined for the local elevator where it will be stored until it is sold according to the farmer's contract.

Left:
A gal's best friend— not diamonds, but her horse—deserves a kiss now and then.

Above:
On a farm that is no longer inhabited, a barn falls into disrepair. The buildings will eventually collapse, as only the crop land is being used.

Right:
Colorful flowering native grasses bloom in the spring outside Toadstool Park in western Nebraska.

CHAPTER ONE

Missouri: Gateway to the West

Echoes of the Civil War

The Civil War, fought from 1861 to 1865, was very divisive in Missouri. Missouri was admitted to the Union as a slave state, but there were many German immigrants in the northern part of the state who opposed slavery. Both sides wanted control of Missouri for the strategic locations on its rivers and railways, and for its natural resources and wealth.

When the war broke out, a special legislature voted to remain with the Union even though the governor was pro-slavery. Forty thousand men enlisted in the Confederate Army; one hundred thousand in the Union, including over eight thousand ex-slaves and free blacks; and fifty thousand men were consigned to the Home Guard.

There was a Civil War in miniature going on in Missouri, and the Home Guard was to protect the citizens from the border wars and insurrections within the state. More than four hundred battles and skirmishes took place in Missouri. Only Virginia and Tennessee sustained heavier fighting during the war.

Families were torn asunder; at the battle of Athens, Colonel Moore of the Union Army fought against his own two sons, who were in the Confederate camp. Bill Quantrill and his raiders, including his protégés Frank and Jesse James and the Younger brothers, led bloody guerrilla raids on Union soldiers and pro-Union citizens during the war, and became notorious bandits after the war. The enmity caused by the war has wounds that exist today in certain parts of Missouri.

Right:
The Civil War battle site at Wilson's Creek National Battlefield is located near Springfield, Missouri.

Left:
Autumn is shown here in full splendor along the banks of the Missouri River near Weston, Missouri.

The Missouri River Confluence

The Missouri River stretches nearly three thousand miles across the plains. The West begins where the Missouri River meets the Mississippi River, just south of St. Louis. Here the Lewis and Clark Park marks the confluence of the two mighty American rivers. The Missouri River, also known as the Great Muddy or Misery, which thwarted so many expectations for an overland river route to the Pacific, now flows noiselessly into the barge-laden Mississippi.

St. Genevieve, south of St. Louis on the Mississippi, was settled by the French in 1735, and has preserved its historical ancestry. Hannibal, north of St. Louis on the Mississippi, was the boyhood home of Samuel Clemens, better known as Mark Twain. His books, such as *Roughing It* and *The Adventures of Huckleberry Finn*, made river-boat travel and adventure part of American mythology.

Ten thousand years ago, the Woodland cultures settled near the Illinois, Mississippi, and Missouri rivers. Nearly twenty thousand Indians lived in Cahokia, Illinois, just east of St. Louis.

North of the Missouri River, Missouri is a glaciated plain with good farm lands. South of the river lie the Ozark highlands, rugged terrain with lead and iron ore deposits. The southern Bootheel area is primeval forest swamp, now used for farming tobacco. The Osage Plain in the west has rolling hills, grasslands, and zinc deposits.

Above:
Near Springfield, Missouri, a farmhouse stands at the scene of a Civil War battle which took place on August 10, 1861; after heavy losses on both sides, the Confederate Army was victorious.

Right:
Near Eminence, Missouri, a historic grist mill is located at Alley Spring. The spring is part of the Ozark National Scenic Riverways, and is a popular spot for canoeing.

Right:
Here, in what is now the Jesse James Bank Museum, in Liberty, Missouri, the James Gang absconded with over $60,000 and killed a young bystander.

Right:
Two farmers take time out from their chores for some camaraderie over a cup of coffee at the local town cafe.

Left:
Fishermen and hikers alike come for the spectacular autumnal sunsets along the Missouri River near Parkville, Missouri.

Left:
Jesse James committed the first daylight bank robbery in America in Liberty, Missouri, on Valentine's Day in 1866.

Right:
Historic Saint Genevieve, founded by French farmers in the 1730s and Missouri's oldest permanent settlement, retains many of its original structures, including this hotel.

Above:
The tool shop where everything was handcrafted for
the pioneers' needs is re-created in Missouri Town, a
mid-nineteenth-century village near Kansas City, Missouri.

Left:
Missouri's history
is etched in the
face of an old mule
skinner named
Clay Clinton, of
Springfield, Missouri.

Following page:
Commemorating St.
Louis as the gateway to the
West, the Gateway Arch,
designed by Eero Saarinen,
was completed in 1965.
A ride to the top provides
panoramic views of
St. Louis, Missouri, and
the Mississippi River.

St. Louis

St. Louis, which lies on the Mississippi River, has a proud history as an important port city. In 1763–64 Pierre Laclede planned for St. Louis to be a trading post twenty miles from the confluence of the Mississippi and Missouri rivers, on a crest of a hill that was relatively safe from flooding. The village was laid out to resemble New Orleans and named for Louis IX, a thirteenth-century crusader king of France. It was the center of the fur trade network in 1764. Lewis and Clark began their expeditions from St. Louis in 1803. Clark became governor of the territory in 1813 and governed until statehood was granted in 1821. After the War of 1812, St. Louis became the "gateway to the West" as mass emigration began.

Today, two and a half million people live in the metropolitan area, and some seven million visit annually. The Gateway Arch, a 630-foot stainless-steel structure created by Eero Saarinen, completed in 1965, serves as a powerful symbol of St. Louis's past as well as present.

Union Station, built in 1894 and once the world's largest railroad center, had its last train pass through in the 1970s. The station, a monument of gold leaf, great halls, and spectacular space, lay dormant for several years. It has since been transformed into a retail shopping complex, hotel, and museum.

Forest Park, thirteen hundred acres on the site of the World's Fair of 1904, is home to the St. Louis Art Museum. The museum was built by renowned architect Cass Gilbert.

The Cathedral of St. Louis, begun in 1907, contains a spectacular collection of mosaic tiles done in Byzantine design. There are over 100 million pieces of mosaic in the interior.

The Botanical Gardens, founded by Henry Shaw in 1859, are the country's oldest public gardens and the institution is an acknowledged leader in botanical research and education.

Down by the waterfront is Laclede's Landing, named for the founder of St. Louis. This collection of brick warehouse buildings on cobblestone streets has been restored and nearby riverboats offer cruises on the mighty Mississippi.

St. Louis, like so many other American cities, has seen its fortunes rise and fall throughout its history, but the spirit of innovation and adventure is alive and well and the city remains a successful symbol of the unification of the past with the present.

Below:
Union Station in St. Louis, Missouri, appears majestic and powerful at night. The *Meeting of the Waters* fountain represents the marriage of the Mississippi and Missouri rivers.

Left:
The Gateway Arch in downtown St. Louis, Missouri, highlights the Mississippi River skyline.

Above:

The interior of the Fox Theater in St. Louis, Missouri, is embellished with Moorish and Indian motifs. This 1929 movie palace has been restored and is home today to many theatrical productions.

Right:

Lionel Hampton and his big band play jazz at the Folly Theatre in Kansas City, Missouri, a restored theater built in 1900.

Left:

This handsome residential home near Lafayette Square in St. Louis was built after the Civil War. The square was the first public park in St. Louis, developed from early French settlers' farms, and soon became a fashionable neighborhood.

Kansas City

The Kansas City area was a main overland trailway to the West. When "manifest destiny," the phrase coined by John Louis O'Sullivan, offered a final stamp of approval to America's quest to conquer the continent, overland trails were utilized to assist expansion.

By 1843 both Independence and Westport had become major hubs due to the opening of both the Oregon Trail and the Santa Fe Trail. John McCoy's settlement, Kansas City, was incorporated by the state of Missouri in 1853; and Kansas City, in turn, annexed Westport in 1889.

Kansas City began to outgrow Independence when the Missouri Pacific Railroad reached Kansas City in 1865. Kansas City opened its first bridge over the Missouri River in 1869, and now could ship goods both east and west.

Today Kansas City, located on the banks of the Kansas and Missouri rivers, is a bi-state metropolitan area on the border of Missouri and Kansas, spread out over rolling hills and bluffs, with a population of one and a half million distributed among many distinct neighborhoods. In the early 1900s, Kansas City jazz developed a distinctive style. It was home to Scott Joplin, Charlie Parker, Count Basie, Joe Turner, and many others.

During the freewheeling Pendergast administration, that spanned both Prohibition and Depression years, Kansas City was a wide-open town, with over two hundred joints playing music day and night. The town shut down when Pendergast was convicted for income tax evasion and it never recovered its momentum. Today, the music scene has begun to revive. Eighteenth Street and Vine is a national historical landmark, and there are weekend jam sessions at the Mutual Musicians Foundation, founded in 1920.

Kansas City is a city with more boulevards than Paris, and more fountains than any city except Rome. One unique area, the Country Club Plaza, is a fifty-five-acre Spanish-style shopping center. Built in 1922, it is the oldest shopping center in the country. Modeled on the city of Seville, Spain, it has fountains, pastel-colored tile-roofed buildings, imported statuary and artwork, mosaics, and ornate towers that create a distinctly European ambiance.

Westport retains its historical roots in the wagon trails and the Civil War. Hallmark Cards has its own city-within-a-city—the eighty-five-acre Crown Center. Since 1840 a City Market has sold produce, flowers, and many other items on weekends.

Kansas City is home to the internationally known Nelson-Atkins Museum of Art. The well-known artist Thomas Hart Benton lived in Kansas City. His works are found in the Nelson-Atkins Museum and the Truman Library features a Benton mural. His residence is maintained by the National Parks Service.

Kansas City, combining its small-town friendliness with a city's sophistication, is one of the most beautiful cities in America.

Below:
One of the many fountains in Country Club Plaza in Kansas City, Missouri, lends an old-world charm to the plaza.

Right:
Rising above the Country Club Plaza in Kansas City, a Spanish tower beckons. The Plaza, built in the 1920s, was modeled on the city of Seville, Spain, and contains nearly 200 shops and restaurants.

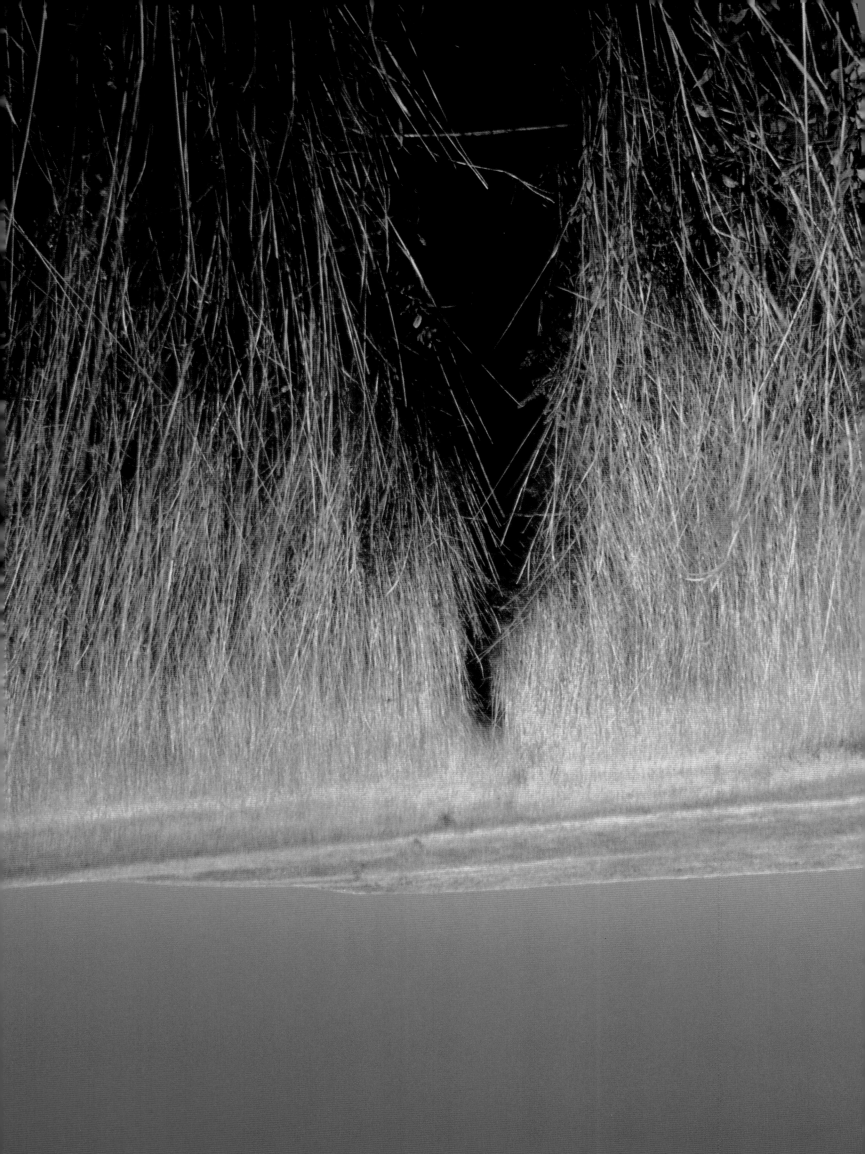

CHAPTER TWO
Kansas:
The Central Plains

Crossroads of the Nation

Eons ago, salty inland seas from the Gulf of Mexico flooded the Kansas Territory; as the seas receded, swamps and flood plains emerged. Ancient chalk pyramids and spires seventy feet in height are visible for miles in the northwest corner of Kansas, fossil-filled monuments from the ancient sea bed. Over the centuries, these strange configurations have served as landmarks for travelers.

In 1541 Coronado, seeking gold in the city of Quivira, came to Kansas. Here he met Wichita, Kaw, and Pawnee Indian tribes. The Pawnee were the largest, numbering nearly twenty-five thousand. Kansas translates as "people of the south wind" in the language of the Kaw, one of the thirty tribes that lived in Kansas. By 1880, the Indians had moved to reservations in Oklahoma; only a few small reservations representing five tribes remain in Kansas today.

With the passage of the Kansas-Nebraska Territorial Act of 1854, pro-slavery and free state supporters began moving into Kansas Territory. The extremists raged on both sides for ten years, causing Kansas to be known as "Bleeding Kansas." In the end most settlers—small farmers who were immigrants from European countries—were opposed to slavery, not on moral grounds but for economic reasons. They feared that they would be unable to compete against slave labor and would lose their own chances for employment. Kansas became a free state in 1861. Many blacks migrated to Kansas in the 1870s from the rural South, where they faced poverty and discrimination. These blacks became known as "exodusters."

Right:
The beautiful Smoky Hills in northern Kansas were formerly a trail route to Denver, Colorado, before the railroads arrived.

Left:
Hikers, botanists, and the public are welcome to enjoy walking the trails through amber-hued grasses in the Konza Prairie Research Center, near Manhattan, Kansas.

The Flint Hills

Kansas has two distinct prairie regions: the Flint Hills and the high plains. The Flint Hills cover 500 million acres of tall-grass prairies, dividing Kansas nearly in half from north to south. Here are the last open cattle ranges, bluestem grasses and wild flowers, and deposits of limestone chert—flint—that give this region its name. The Konza Prairie is the largest extant tall-grass prairie in the United States, comprising some 8,616 acres in the Flint Hills region.

The town of Cottonwood Falls is noted for the Chase County Courthouse, which was carved from native limestone, a Second Empire structure with black walnut interior. It remains the oldest working courthouse in the state. Council Grove was a major staging point for wagon trains embarking on the Santa Fe Trail and Emporia became known for its outstanding newspaperman William Allen White, editor of the *Emporia Gazette*.

Other towns such as Dunlap, settled mostly by freed exodusters, who were barred from Emporia and Cottonwood Falls, had robust beginnings, but the end of the cattle drives, the loss of railroad stations, and the Great Depression of the 1930s reduced its population to the point where it lives on mostly in memory.

Above:
Monument Rocks, in northwest Kansas, are ancient chalk bluffs and spires, vestiges of the great inland sea that covered the Great Plains eons ago.

Right:
Cottonwood Falls, Kansas, is home to the Chase County Courthouse. Designed in 1873, this Second Empire structure is the oldest Kansan courthouse still in use.

Wild West Country

Western Kansas is the high plains—dry, dusty, wind-scorched land, rutted from the millions of longhorn cattle driven up from Texas. Cowtown after cowtown, the raucous and the wild, were created by the drives—first Abilene, then Wichita, and finally Dodge City, in the westernmost part of the state. The plains are rutted also with the wheels of wagons, four abreast as they traversed the Santa Fe Trail, traveling 550 miles through Kansas. Millions of dollars in trade was made annually along the Santa Fe Trail.

The railroads owned ten million acres of land in Kansas and they needed settlers and workers. They advertised in foreign newspapers and soon one in ten settlers came from abroad. Swedish, German, and Russian emigrants settled in central Kansas. The Mennonites, a pacifist group from Russia, emigrated and brought with them a hard, red winter wheat—turkey red. This became the gold Coronado was looking for. Kansas, with its golden fields of grain, is the top wheat-producing state in the Union. The Kansas Pacific and the Atchison, Topeka & Santa Fe Railroads laid their tracks through Kansas in the 1870s. The era of overland coaches, Pony Express, and wagon trains was at an end.

Buffalo Bill Cody was one of the most respected Pony Express riders when he was just fifteen years old. He also had a reputation for being an outstanding buffalo hunter, killing

Above:
Front Street of the 1870s has been re-created as a museum of the authentic history of Dodge City, Kansas. Melodramas, medicine shows, gunfights, and more are today's summer entertainment.

Right:
A monument to the gunfighters of the Old West is found in Dodge City, Kansas.

nearly five thousand buffalo in less than a year to feed the railroad workers laying tracks. Buffalo were hunted for their hides and, with the Army's encouragement, in order to hasten the demise of the Indians.

James Butler, a.k.a. Wild Bill Hickok, nearly lost an arm through an encounter with a grizzly bear when he was a Raton Pass stage driver on the Santa Fe Trail. He later became a gunfighter and a famous sheriff. Wyatt Earp and Bat Masterson were sheriffs of Dodge City. In 1892, residents of Coffeyville thwarted the Dalton gang's plan to rob two banks, and killed the robbers. Their outlines are painted on the streets outside the Coffeyville Bank, and the Dalton Museum retells their exploits.

Dodge City was built on a bluff overlooking the Arkansas River, on the Santa Fe Trail. For ten years it was a wild cowtown. In 1877 there were sixteen saloons in a town with less than a thousand residents. Boot Hill Cemetery was established to bury those that were killed, usually in gunfights, who had no families to give them proper burials in Fort Dodge Cemetery. Most were buried with their boots on, and often wolves dug up the bodies after the burials. Alice Chambers, a "soiled dove," was the last person buried there, in 1878. The last cattle drive into Dodge City occurred in 1885. The quarantine denying entrance to Texas longhorns and the diseases they carried had finally reached Dodge, and its heyday was ended.

Today, Dodge City boasts a bronze oversize longhorn on its main street and, in its re-creation of its past, entertains summer visitors with gunfights and salon chanteuses in its Boot Hill Museum and Cemetery, with the Long Branch Saloon as the star venue.

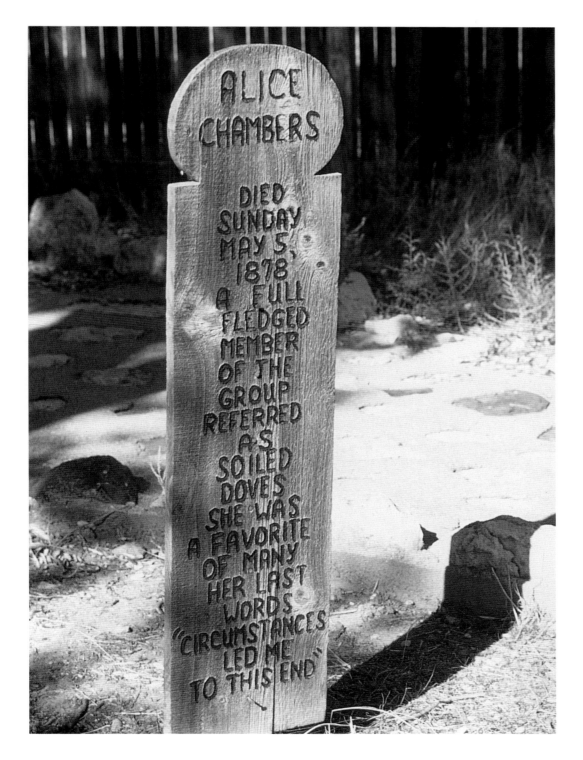

Left:

In Boot Hill Cemetery, Dodge City, Kansas, a wooden marker tells a story. This cemetery was created for the folks who died—mostly with their boots on—during gun fights, and had no kin to bury them in the proper cemetery at Fort Dodge.

Above:
Old Cowtown
Museum re-creates
the old cattle town
of Wichita, Kansas,
during the 1860s
and 1870s.

Left:
Over a hot forge,
a blacksmith
demonstrates
his horseshoe-
making craft.

Abilene and Wichita

Abilene was the first of the famous Kansas cowtowns, and the first to die. In 1867 this tiny frontier village was transformed into a major cattle town as the cattle drives reached Kansas. Over a five-year period, more than three million head of cattle were driven along the Chisholm Trail from Texas to Abilene. In 1872 farmers moved in and began fencing in the range. Barbed wire was fought with bullets by the cattle barons.

Dwight David Eisenhower is Abilene's most famous citizen and Wild Bill Hickok its most notorious. The Eisenhower Center contains the presidential library and museum, the president's boyhood home, and his and his wife Mamie's gravesites. Abilene also has a reconstructed Old Abilene Town and Western Museum, complete with shootouts along its famous Texas Street, and drinks are available at Marshall Wild Bill's favorite hangout, the Alamo Saloon.

The city of Wichita was built on Wichita Indian land. They were forced to leave their homelands in 1867 and pushed southward to Oklahoma and Texas. The railroad arrived in 1872, and for three years Wichita became a boom cattle town. The town, with a population of three thousand, made three thousand dollars a month from licensing fees on gambling, alcohol, and prostitution. Children went to school by day in buildings that were used as brothels by night. After three heady years, the quarantine against Texas longhorns effectively ended Wichita's reign as a wild and woolly cowtown. The reform movement in 1880 brought prohibition, and Wichita sought to diversify its businesses.

Today, some four hundred thousand people live in Wichita, the largest city in Kansas, home to such diverse industries as Cessna, Learjet, Beechcraft, and Pizza Hut. Old Cowtown, a reconstruction of historic Wichita, thrives as a major tourist attraction. Wichita's heritage is commemorated by a sixty-foot sculpture of the Indian "Keeper of the Plains" that graces Wichita's Mid-America All Indian Center along the banks of the confluence of the Big and Little Arkansas rivers.

Below:

The former City Hall of Wichita, Kansas, built in 1892, is now home to the Wichita-Sedwick County Historical Museum.

Right:

Open for tours, the Lebold-Vahsholtz Mansion, an Italianate structure built in Abilene, Kansas, in 1880, has been restored to its former splendor.

CHAPTER THREE

Nebraska: Land of Western Trails

Legacy of the Pioneers

Nebraska has long been a watering hole, a place along the way to somewhere else. This is the heart of the "Great American Desert," a phrase coined by Major Long in the early 1800s, an appellation that remained as pioneers traveled along the Platte River en route to Oregon, Utah, California, Colorado, and South Dakota. The Platte, a wide, sandy expanse of water, runs length-wise through the state.

The Oto Indian word "Ni Blathka" means "flat water," and this phrase evolved into "Nebraska." The Pawnee were the dominant Indian tribe in the 1800s. They were avid traders with other Indian nations and with the Spanish and Mexicans of Santa Fe. Through contact with the whites, many Pawnee died of smallpox and cholera in the 1830s. In 1875 they gave up their remaining lands to the United States and moved to Oklahoma.

Fur traders followed Lewis and Clark along the Missouri River, and traders for John Jacob Astor traveled the length of the Platte River in 1812. In 1830 Jedediah Smith, William Sublette, and David Jackson led the first wagon train along the Platte. Soon more settlers and gold seekers came. Between 1841 and 1866, over half a million travelers passed through Nebraska along the Oregon and Mormon trails. The Oregon Trail was the longest wagon trail in history, stretching some two thousand miles.

Right:
The railroads cross through the Sand Hills in Nebraska, carrying coal and other products.

Left:
This covered wagon or prairie schooner sits by the Oregon Trail site at Scotts Bluff, Nebraska.

In 1854, fewer than twenty-five hundred people lived in Nebraska, but the Homestead Act of 1860 and the railroads attracted so many settlers and workers that the population rose to nearly a million by 1890. In 1980 the population was 1.5 million. The two major railroads, the Union Pacific and the Burlington, received seven million acres of land from the government to build their tracks through Nebraska.

Both the Pulitzer Prize–winning novelist Willa Cather and the historian Mari Sandoz have written eloquently about living on the plains. Willa Cather's home town of Red Cloud in the Republican River Valley has preserved her home and several other buildings that were prominent in her novels, including the acclaimed *My Antonia*.

Nebraska has the distinction of being the first state where women won the right to own property and the right to pursue higher education. Nebraska was also the first plains state that granted voting rights to women.

Below:
Toadstool Park,
in the Badlands
of western Nebraska,
has a lunarlike
landscape.

Above:
Chimney Rock, a
450-foot spire, was
a famous landmark
along the Oregon Trail.

Left:
When Mormon pioneers
camped in Omaha, Nebraska,
from 1846 to 1847, they lived
in sod houses and traveled by
covered wagon; these historical
items are kept at the Mormon
Pioneer visitor center.

The Sand Hills

The Sand Hills are the largest area of sand dunes in the western hemisphere. Here sand dunes, covered with prairie grass undulating like ocean waves, cover eighteen thousand square miles in northwest Nebraska. This is cattle country, and working windmills dot the landscape, providing well water for the herds.

Along the southern edge of the Sand Hills are several eroded buttes and mesas that served as markers for travelers along the Oregon and Mormon trails. Chimney Rock is a spire that rises 450 feet almost out of nowhere and Scotts Bluff, an 810-foot-high butte, is thought to be at least 14 million years old. Eerie sculpturelike deposits of clay and sandstone sediment rise up out of the plains to greet the traveler, ancient remains from the ocean floor that once covered these Great Plains.

Trails West

The Pine Ridge area in the far west was home to Sioux Indians under Chief Red Cloud. Fort Robinson was created in 1874 to keep the Indians under surveillance, and it was here that the Oglala Sioux war chief Crazy Horse, who had come to the fort with nine hundred Indians to surrender in 1877, was arrested on orders from General George Crook; the Indian leader was knifed to death shortly after his arrest. Fort Robinson is now a state park, with museums, historical activities, guest lodging, and other amenities for summer visitors.

Outside of Alliance, Nebraska, stands a bizarre piece of sculpture called Carhenge, built in 1987 by Jim Reinders, and patterned after the ancient, mystical Stonehenge of England. Cars, sandblasted gray, have been arranged in a circle and topped with additional cars to resemble Stonehenge. Recently on the day of the summer solstice people celebrated the occasion with great cheer by staging pageants, feasting, and building a huge bonfire.

Bancroft is the home of the Neihardt Center, named for John Neihardt, Nebraska's Poet Laureate in Perpetuity. He died in 1973, at age ninety-two. His major work, *A Cycle of the West*, was written over a twenty-nine-year period. The center's grounds include the Sioux Prayer Garden, a symbol of the Hoop of the World, described to Neihardt by the Oglala Sioux Holy Man Black Elk in their book *Black Elk Speaks*.

The Buffalo Bill Ranch in North Platte, Nebraska, now a state historical park, was the ranch of Buffalo Bill Cody, the former buffalo hunter, Pony Express rider, and, later, showman par excellence. His famous Wild West Show traveled the country and abroad from 1883 to 1913. His show helped create many legendary myths about the American West. For many people, these performances became the truth about the so-called Wild West. Annie Oakley, an exciting trick-shot performer, was part of the

Below:
In 1868 the historic Muir home in Brownville, Nebraska, was built of native brick in the Italianate style.

Right:
The river town of Brownville, Nebraska, was once a bustling steamboat landing and ferry crossing; now it's a charming historic village.

Above:
The summer solstice is celebrated with a bonfire at Carhenge, outside Alliance, Nebraska.

Left:
Modern Druids perform a solstice pageant at Carhenge, where new age meets the stone age.

Left:
Will McBride, a cowboy artist, displays a piece of baling wire sculpture from an exhibition in Kearny, Nebraska.

Following page:
Hay bales, some shaped like loaves of bread, are a constant presence throughout the plains.

troop. Even the great Indian chief Sitting Bull traveled with Buffalo Bill's entourage of trick riders and sharp shooters. Authentic props were used, including real buffalo, further enhancing the show's air of credibility.

Omaha and Lincoln

Omaha, on the western bank of the Missouri, is a Maha Indian word meaning "those going against the current." Lewis and Clark reached the Omaha area in 1804, followed by Manuel de Lisa, founder of the Missouri Fur Company, who installed a trading post in 1813. Omaha became the last stop on the Mormon Trail to buy supplies for the trip across the Great Plains, and wagons were backed up for six weeks waiting to cross the Missouri River.

In 1863 the Union Pacific made Omaha/Council Bluffs the eastern terminus of its coast-to-coast railroad. In 1869 the Union Pacific met the Central Pacific, and the famous golden spike was driven into the tracks, celebrating the completion of the transcontinental railroad. The Union Stockyards opened in 1884, becoming the main economic force in Omaha.

There are approximately 350 thousand residents living in Omaha at this time. Omaha has retained its status as a major livestock market; it is the fourth-largest meat processing center in the country. It is also a major food processing center: San Giorgio produces 54 million tons of pasta a year using 1.2 million tons of Nebraskan wheat, and Kellogg's ships nine thousand railroad carloads of cereal made from Nebraskan corn yearly.

The Great Plains Black Museum documents black history on the plains. Their collection includes photographs of the cowboy Nat Love and the black militia, known as "buffalo soldiers" (an Indian term for black soldiers). The Western Heritage Museum is located in the spectacular art deco–style Union Pacific Station. The Joslyn Art Museum, an art deco building in pink

Below:

The downtown Omaha, Nebraska, skyline is seen at twilight from the Central Park Mall. Here stands the Woodmen Insurance building, flanked by the AT&T and ConAgra corporate headquarters.

Right:
Historic Trinity Cathedral, a Gothic Revival structure, was built in 1883 in Omaha, Nebraska.

marble, houses the internationally known Maximillian/Bodner collection of early-nineteenth-century American Indian culture.

The General Crook House Museum in Fort Omaha was once used by the general, a Civil War officer and Indian fighter from 1878 to 1888. He entertained presidents and other dignitaries in his home, where his skill in taxidermy is marked by the profuse number of wild animals on display in his den.

The Old Market, built in the 1880s to outfit and supply western pioneers, is a collection of Italianate buildings on cobblestone streets. In the 1960s, artists and craftspeople began moving in, opening studios and galleries. Soon restaurants and boutiques followed, and this section of the city became vibrant and alive with creativity and culture. Once again, the past was reborn as a new kind of pioneer moved into these warehouse lofts.

Lincoln, the state capital, lies about thirty miles west of Omaha. The Capitol, known as the Tower of the Plains, rises four hundred feet in the air, and cost ten million dollars to build in 1922. Interior artwork centers on the themes of Nebraska's Indian heritage and its agrarian pioneers.

William Jennings Bryan, the Populist orator and presidential candidate, was Lincoln, Nebraska's, most celebrated citizen.

The Sheldon Memorial Art Gallery, a white marble box designed by architect Philip Johnson, sits on the University of Nebraska campus, and contains many important pieces of twentieth-century American art.

Lincoln has its renovated "Haymarket" district, with turn-of-the-century brick warehouses that now house restaurants, galleries, and other unique shops. The National Museum of Roller Skating, the only one in the world, is right here in Lincoln, with a collection of over twelve hundred skates and skating artifacts.

Below:
The Joslyn Art Museum, built in 1931 in Omaha, Nebraska, is a fine example of Art Deco design.

Left:
This bronze statue in the Mormon Pioneer Cemetery was erected in memory of the Mormons who made Omaha their winter camp for two years, where more than 600 settlers died from typhoid and other diseases.

Above:
The ivory-colored
terra-cotta exterior
of the former Union
Station, in Omaha,
Nebraska, is a fine
example of the stream-
lined Art Deco style.

Left:
Omaha's Union Station,
erected in 1931, is now
the home of the Western
Heritage Museum, where
the city's growth from
1880 to 1954 is detailed.

Right:
Behind the statue of
Abraham Lincoln rises
the Tower of the Plains,
the state capitol building
at Lincoln, Nebraska.

CHAPTER FOUR

Iowa: Tall-Grass Prairie

Harvest of the Past

Iowa is located between two major American rivers: the Mississippi River forms its eastern border and the Missouri River is its western border. In between the rivers is some of the most fertile land in the nation.

The last major glaciers passed through Iowa approximately twelve thousand years ago, leaving a gently rolling terrain and a deep sediment bed. Here the tall prairie grasses took root, covering eighty-five percent of the land. The grasses, with deep root structures, built up nutrients in the soil and grew undisturbed for eight thousand years. When white settlers arrived 150 years ago, they were met with a sea of grass, six to eight feet in height, for as far as they could see.

The challenge to domesticate the land was taken up, and the sod-busters broke the prairies' thick mantle with their plows, finally clearing the state of prairie lands. Today fewer than five thousand acres of native prairie exists.

Plowing up the prairie has resulted in Iowa's being the number-one state in corn production, second in soybeans, and first in livestock marketing. One-tenth of the nation's food supply comes from Iowa, where three out of four acres are used as crop land. But not without cost. Some 260 million tons of topsoil are lost annually, most of it running into the rivers.

Right:
The Anderson Prairie, one of the few remaining native prairies, is a protected preserve outside Estherville, Iowa.

Left:
Iowa prairie grasses bend in the winter wind before the snow falls.

The Indian inhabitants whom the settlers first encountered were the Ioway, who sold their lands and moved west in 1838. The Sauk and Mesquakie lived in southern Iowa along the Mississippi River. They left unwillingly in 1832, but a small tribe of Mesquakie bought three thousand acres of land in the 1850s near Tama, and a thousand Indians still live on the tribal lands. This is the site of annual powwows, where Indian people gather to celebrate their culture with song and dance.

Iowa became a free state in 1846, and many Iowans were active in hiding runaway slaves in the "underground railroad." In 1856, Congress gave four million acres of Iowa land to the railroads as an encouragement to lay tracks through Iowa. By 1880 five major railroad lines ran through the state. The freight trains carried grain, ore, and other agricultural products to markets.

During hard times, men would ride the rails across the country, looking for work. Since 1900 Britt, Iowa, has been the home of the nationally renowned Hobo Convention, held annually in August. Colorful characters, both men and women, camp out for several days, elect a king and queen of the hoboes, and have an old-fashioned get-together, swapping stories of lives lived on the rails.

Above:
Norman Blass, a farmer, surveys the half-million-bushel overflow of corn at the Dolliver, Iowa, elevator.

Right:
A "king of the road" comes to partake of the festivities at the annual Hobo Days celebration in Britt, Iowa, a tradition since 1900.

Above:
Spring wildflowers
bloom amidst a
grove of trees in
West Bend, Iowa.

Left:
Flower beds planted
along old railroad lines
enliven the Golden
Sun Feed Elevator
in Estherville, Iowa.

Left:
Dorothy Blass, of
Estherville, Iowa,
is known for her
colorful gardens
and here enjoys her
brightly blooming
peony bushes.

River Towns in Iowa

The French explorers Marquette and Jolliet reached Iowa in 1673 during their exploration of the Mississippi River. They were followed by Julien Dubuque, who began mining lead in 1788 and founded the town named after him. Dubuque became a busy river port with lumber and lead shipped down the Mississippi. The town became quite prosperous in the late 1800s, and this led to the construction of many architecturally distinguished buildings.

The Dubuque Museum of Art is housed in the Old Jail, a rare specimen of Egyptian Revivalist architecture, built in 1857 from native limestone and cast iron. Many Victorian mansions, such as the Redstone, have been restored, and serve as bed-and-breakfast inns. The Fenelon Place Elevator, built in 1882, is a short, steep ride to the top of the bluffs, where one can see the borders of Illinois, Wisconsin, and Iowa. Riverboat gambling has been revived, and floating casinos traverse the Mississippi on daily cruises.

On the western side of the state lies Sioux City, on the confluence of the Big Sioux, Floyd, and Missouri rivers. Chief War Eagle of the Sioux settled there in 1849 with his daughter and son-in-law, a French Canadian trader named Theophile Bruguier. War Eagle's presence eased the way for white settlement. He is remembered with a memorial built on his grave site on a bluff overlooking the Missouri River.

The railroads arrived in 1868 and soon Sioux City became a large meat-packing center. The Woodbury County Courthouse is an important structure in early-twentieth-century design. Its basic form is Prairie Style architecture, developed by Frank Lloyd Wright. This style reflects the rolling prairies, with gently sloping roofs and sheltering overhangs.

Following page:
Two grain bins sit in a silent, snow-covered field under a setting winter sun in Iowa.

Right:
The Dubuque Casino Belle, a casino gambling riverboat, travels the Mississippi River near Dubuque, Iowa, on daily excursions.

Left:
Little Sioux Lutheran Church sits on a country road near Milford, Iowa. Farm families in the area have been coming here for four to five generations.

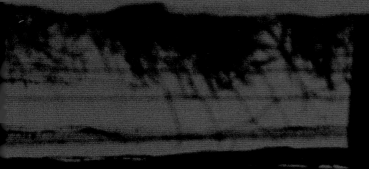

Left:
Summer's pleasures
at West Okoboji Lake
in Iowa are enjoyed
by these vacationers
riding a banana-
shaped float pulled
by a power boat.

Iowa's Great Lakes

As the result of glacial movement in Iowa twelve thousand years ago, certain depressions became lakes and water-filled natural basins with no drainage. A series of ten lakes, called Iowa's great lakes—Spirit Lake, West and East Okoboji, and Big Spirit are the largest of the ten—were considered sacred lakes by the Sioux. In 1856 the Sioux chieftain Inkpaduta attacked a settlement of whites on Spirit Lake, killing some thirty homesteaders in revenge for the death of his brother some years earlier. The site of the attack, the Gardner Cabin, is now a national parks monument in Arnolds Park, and its legacy of violence has yielded to the site of the Great Lakes Amusement Park, complete with an old-fashioned wooden roller coaster.

Right:
April Palmer takes
her young son
Dustin for his
first ride sledding
in the snow, a
frequent pastime.

Left:
Lidtke Mill, on Lime
Springs in eastern
Iowa, now houses
antiques and contains
its original machinery,
including a working
generator and turbine.

Right:
Built in 1918, the Woodbury County Courthouse in Sioux City, Iowa, is an important piece of Prairie Style architecture. The prairie style, developed by Frank Lloyd Wright, was primarily used in residences rather than public buildings.

Right:
A patriotic rodeo clown entertains spectators at the Fourth of July festival in Armstrong, Iowa.

Left:
Memorial Day is celebrated on the town square in Estherville, Iowa.

Left:
The All American Trick Riders entertain a crowd at the annual Sidney, Iowa, rodeo.

Above:

Winter's cold is reflected
in this farm scene in
rural northwest Iowa.

Below:

This young lad is smiling
because this classic 1934
Ford belonging to his
father will someday be his.

Where the Tall Corn Grows

*We're from I-oway, I-oway, Land of all the Lands, Joy on every Hand,
We're from Ioway, Ioway, That's Where the Tall Corn Grows!*

This is the song my brothers and I sang when we traveled to Minnesota to see relatives, shouting it out lustily from the car windows as we entered a foreign state. Of course, the landscape between northern Iowa and southern Minnesota was virtually the same, and only a state roadside sign welcomed you into another territory. Yet we felt an incredible loyalty to our own state.

Though I've lived in New York City for nearly twenty years, Iowa is home. I am one of those statistics cited that show a decline in rural population; a child of a farm family who leaves the state to find a career elsewhere. My immediate family lives in Iowa; parents, brothers, children, and grandchildren. My father, Norman Blass, is eighty-two, born in 1913; my mother, Dorothy, is seventy-nine. Their story is like that of so many other pioneers.

By 1920 over half the farm families in Iowa were of German descent. Dad's family emigrated from Germany, mother's from Norway. They met at a church social in Spencer, Iowa, and married in 1938. From the time he was six years old, Dad worked on his father's farm, planting and picking corn by hand, driving horses, and doing other tasks. He was the oldest of a family of six children, four girls and two boys.

One of his earliest memories is of a teacher asking when they would come to school. He walked a mile daily to and from the one-room school, through eighth grade, and then he worked full time. When he was a teenager during the Depression, he went to the Red River Valley in North Dakota to find harvest work. He pitchforked wheat into hay racks for threshing and picked potatoes for two cents a bushel, each bushel weighing about eighty pounds. He slept in farmers' haylofts and they would feed him. Come fall, he returned to Iowa for the corn harvest.

When he and my mother married, his parents gave them four cows, and her parents gave them forty-five chickens. Mom would gather eggs, sell them in town on Fridays for $2.50, and buy all their groceries for the coming week with her egg money. She also had a huge garden, and canned and preserved vegetables for the winter. Eventually, they saved enough money to make a down payment on their own farm. Through hard work, skill, determination, and frugality, they prospered. My father won many awards for the high yields in his fields. He still works and has the constitution of a much younger man. Now it is my brother Randy who does the farming on our family farm. His young sons are eager to help him drive the tractor and do chores. There is a bond that comes from working land that has been passed down from generation to generation.

Right:

An annual classic-car show in
Armstrong, Iowa, draws a big
crowd. It is part of their lively
Independence Day celebrations.

CHAPTER FIVE

South Dakota: The Western Plains

Native American Ancestral Voices

Woodland people moved into South Dakota from the east nearly two thousand years ago. They farmed, lived in earth lodges, made pottery, and raised corn. Over time, they evolved into the Arikara Indians, who lived along the Missouri River and who were the most dominant tribe until the mid-1700s, when they were surpassed in strength and size by the Sioux.

The Sioux became known as bold, fierce plains warriors, feared by other tribes. Within their own clans, the Sioux taught generosity, and people in need were not refused. A man could not grow rich, because he gave away all that he had. When he died, his possessions were given away; thus his children did not inherit material wealth.

By contrast, possessions and property were paramount to the white man. Accordingly, in 1874, when General Custer entered the Black Hills and discovered gold, pandemonium arose among the whites, who then wanted the Indians dislodged. In June of 1876 the Indians, led by Sitting Bull and Crazy Horse, defeated Custer in the infamous Battle of Little Big Horn. This victory was short-lived. The army moved mercilessly against the Indians, and the U.S. government forced them to cede their rights to the Black Hills in September of 1876.

In 1889 another treaty took more lands from the Sioux. In 1890, the death of Sitting Bull and the Massacre at Wounded Knee signaled a final defeat for the great Sioux Nation. The government then tried to assimilate the Sioux and other Indians into white culture. Every detail of Indian

Right:
Petroglyphs, or picture writings, made by early Native Americans are found in the Red Rock Canyon near Hot Springs, South Dakota.

Left:
The Badlands National Park of South Dakota is an ancient landscape of sandstone, spires, and precipices formed by wind and water erosion.

culture and identity was to be eradicated. This policy proved to be an abysmal failure. Despite the past, Sioux culture and values survive.

At present, some fifty thousand Sioux Indians live on nine reservations. Some reservations, like the Santee Sioux at Flandreau, have prospered. Here I was privileged to meet Harvey and Agnes Ross, both nearly eighty years old. Their pasts included going to reservation schools and going on to become educators themselves. Agnes has a Master's Degree, and she has taught and written poetry for many years. She was the first woman to serve on the tribal council; today, her granddaughter does so. Harvey is an artist and craftsman of unparalleled degree. Their eldest son, Dr. A. C. Ross (Ehanamani), is the author of the highly acclaimed book, *We Are All One.*

Today, in attempts to heal the past, Indian culture is openly acknowledged and admired. Indian rituals are celebrated, and powwows are held annually to celebrate a rich past and a hope-filled future.

Below:
Sunset warms
the grassy buttes
in the Badlands
of South Dakota.

Above:
A dancer shakes an eagle spirit stick during
the Black Hills and Northern Plains Indian
Powwow held in Rapid City, South Dakota.

The Black Hills

"Paha Sapa," the Sioux name for the Black Hills, were Indians' sacred grounds. Here medicine men would retreat to fast and pray for spiritual guidance for their tribe. After gold was discovered, miners started pouring in. Homestake Mine, in Lead, purchased by George Hearst (of the Hearst Publishing Empire) in 1877, sat on the mother lode. Now, Homestake is the largest gold mine in the Western Hemisphere; 150 tons of ore are taken out annually. It takes five tons of ore to produce one ounce of gold. Hard-rock miners work in shafts at temperatures of 130 degrees and in tunnels eight thousand feet in depth.

Nearby Deadwood was once one of the most famous mining towns. Seventy-six saloons dotted the streets, and dance-hall and "upstairs" girls arrived in 1876. The rough-and-tumble town welcomed many legends of the West. It was here that Wild Bill Hickok was shot in the back as he sat playing poker, holding two pairs: black aces and eights, which became known as "dead man's hand." Calamity Jane, South Dakota's most notorious woman—a hard-drinking gun-slinger and an army scout—claimed to be his lover, and years later she was buried beside him in Mount Moriah Cemetery.

Today, summer visitors can gamble once again in Deadwood's casinos and can participate in the reenactment of the trial of Jack McCall for the murder of Wild Bill Hickok.

Spearfish Canyon, in the northern Black Hills, is spectacularly beautiful; ponderosa pines, magnificent waterfalls, and rocky vistas abound. The town of Spearfish is the home of the Black Hills Passion Play, the 1906 Matthews Opera House, and the historic Booth Fish Hatchery.

Picturesque Hot Springs is the southern gateway to the Black Hills. The former spa town, built along the Fall River Canyon, has architecturally interesting Richardson Romanesque buildings of native sandstone. The style is known for its massive forms, rounded arches, towers, and rough-

Above:
Needles Highway in Custer State Park, South Dakota, is a spectacular fourteen-mile drive through the granite mountainside.

Right:
Thousands of sightseers come to the Corvette Classic Car Rally at Spearfish, South Dakota, where over 500 Corvette owners from around the nation gather annually for a weekend of events, including Vette Street USA, as seen here from above.

stone masonry. The Mammoth Site is an ancient sink-hole, where over forty Columbian mammoth fossils were unearthed in a Hot Springs housing development excavation.

The Black Hills are filled with attractions: Mount Rushmore, the Crazy Horse Memorial, the Reptile Gardens, Custer Park, Wind Cave, Needles Highway, and much more. The gold is in tourist dollars, and people come by the millions to enjoy these once-sacred mountains.

Living on the Land

In 1889 South Dakota became the fortieth state. About seven hundred thousand people live in South Dakota, including fifty thousand Sioux. Dakotah is a Sioux word, meaning friends. South Dakota is the number-one producer in the United States of oats and rye, second in flax, third in honey and sunflowers, and fourth in spring wheat.

Left:
George Washington is one of four presidents carved onto Mount Rushmore in South Dakota by Gutzon Borglum, completed in 1941. Each presidential face is 60 feet high; Thomas Jefferson, Theodore Roosevelt, and Abraham Lincoln fill out this epic sculpture.

Above:
The southern Black Hills around Hot Springs, South Dakota, abound with intensely hued red-rock canyons, topped with native pines.

Following page:
Looking like confectioner's sugar, a coating of ice covers everything—trees, grasses, fences—near Mitchell, South Dakota, during a winter-wonderland storm.

Above:
One of South Dakota's most famous and beloved architectural landmarks is the Corn Palace in Mitchell, an exhibition hall and auditorium that dates back to 1892, which is redecorated yearly with thousands of bushels of corn and native grasses.

Left:
Chapel in the Hills in Rapid City, South Dakota, is a replica of an 830-year-old Norwegian church.

The Flood Control Act of 1944 created four big dams on the Missouri. This resulted in the loss of most of the original riverbed, and permanent flooding of more than eighty percent of Missouri River bottom lands. Gone are cottonwood forests and thousands of acres of cropland and pasture. Gone also are the ancestral homes of many, both Indian and white. In exchange for this, South Dakotans got flood control, powerful dams that generate electricity, and four large lakes used for fishing and other recreational activities. Agriculture remains the leading industry, with tourism second.

The landscape of South Dakota is a study in contrasts: rugged hills and mountains in the west; rolling plains along the Missouri River that bisect the state in half at Chamberlain; the fertile farm valleys in the east. Sioux Falls, in the east, is the largest city in the state, with a population of 101,000. Here is located the Old Minnehaha County Courthouse Museum, a large Romanesque building housing an extensive collection of pioneer and plains Indians exhibitions. Mitchell is home to one of South Dakota's famous landmarks, the Corn Palace. Each year the facade changes, covered with murals made from local corn and grasses.

The recently produced epic movie *Dances with Wolves* was set in South Dakota emphasizing this land's natural beauty and power seemingly beyond the ken of man.

Wild Horse Sanctuary

Outside Hot Springs is the Wild Horse Sanctuary, run by Dayton Hyde, ranch-er, author, environmentalist. In 1988 he made it his mission to try to find a way to save the wild mustangs that were dying in government feedlots. He was able to persuade the Bureau of Land Management to let him care for a herd of three hundred mustangs. That was the beginning of the sanctuary, now home to near-ly two thousand wild horses.

Many consider Hyde to be a present-day western hero. He has dedicated his life to preserving and caring for these animals that everyone else seemed to have forgotten.

I wrote the following poem after meeting Hyde in 1991:

DAYTON, KEEPER OF THE WILD HORSES

Physically, I remember a big man. Flash of skin
between his jeans and jacket as he bent to close
the fence behind us. An outdoor man, secure in
his passion, a dream vaster than a single person.

Securing a vast land, with slices of red rock canyons
and gorges and easy rolling prairies to feed his passion,
his herd of unwanted mustangs
hundreds of wild mares rescued from destruction.

The untamed animal spirit given its freedom
as he gave up his land
to build a sanctuary for these creatures
whose caretaking he's taken on
rescuing a piece of our forgotten heritage,
insisting on a morality that refutes
that which uses and discards without
a second thought.

He knows them all and they feed each other.
The spirit grows strong.

Black, white, chestnut, roan, pinto, appaloosa, buckskin,
the colors of the western land
that once was theirs when there was no price on it.
They run together, biting, kicking, nuzzling,
reclaiming their past.

There is fundraising and feeding to be done.

And this is where he belongs,
being with the wildness, writing his books,
tending the spirits
in the almost limitless expanse of this sanctuary,
his haven,
Each day driven by the dream.

Right:
Dayton Hyde among
some of the rescued
mustangs on the Wild
Horse Sanctuary in Hot
Springs, South Dakota.

Left:
A participant takes aim in the ax-throwing contest during the Heart of the Hills Logging Show in Hill City, South Dakota.

Left:
Loggers show off their skills and compete during Hill City's logging show, held annually during July in the heart of South Dakota's logging region.

Right:
A bridge spans the Missouri River at Chamberlain, South Dakota. Two Native American Reservations are located nearby: the Crow Creek Sioux and the Lower Brule Sioux. The Missouri River area was always home to numerous Indian nations.

CHAPTER SIX

North Dakota: Missouri River Plains

Frontier Memories

In North Dakota dry winds have sculpted buttes, hogbacks, and mesas from land that once was the ocean's floor. The deep gorge of the Missouri River marks the edge of the glaciers that covered most of the territory twelve thousand years ago. To the east are tall-grass prairies of bluestem, switch grass, and Indian grass. West of the Missouri the land rises, becoming high plateaus that stretch to the Rockies. Here the land is arid, and the prairie is short grass: needle-and-thread, western wheat grass, blue gramma, and upland sedges.

Woodland Indians were early settlers here—mound-building farmers raising corn, sunflowers, and tobacco by the year 600 B.C. Mandans migrated from Minnesota around 1000 A.D. The Hidatsa settled along the Missouri River near the Mandans in the 1600s. The Arikara had begun moving into Mandan Territory in the 1400s. The three tribes lived agriculturally, housing themselves in earth lodges, hunting bison, fishing, and using tublike boats called bull boats to cross the Missouri River.

In 1738 the first contact between Mandans and whites was recorded. Europeans started trading with Indians, but as a result of this contact the Indians were infected with epidemics of smallpox in 1781 and again in 1837 that nearly wiped out the Mandan tribe. In the mid-1700s, the neighboring Sioux also attacked the Mandans, further decimating the tribe. Finally they moved to the confluence of the Knife and Missouri rivers.

Today, the Knife River Indian Villages National Historic Site is an important area of archaeological research. These tribes are known as the Three Affiliated Tribes. During the summer, cel-

Right:
Here a modern-day ranch lies in the heart of the Little Missouri River Valley near Bowman, North Dakota.

Left:
The Theodore Roosevelt National Park preserves some of the most spectacular Badlands of North Dakota.

ebrations and demonstrations of Indian culture are held here. There are some thirty thousand Indians currently living in North Dakota, including the Sioux and Chippewa.

In 1804 Lewis and Clark wintered along the Missouri River with the Mandans. Here they met Sakakawea, the Shoshone woman who at age sixteen and pregnant agreed to be their guide. In the spring she, her husband, and her newly born baby set off with the explorers. She was their guide and interpreter, bought horses for them, and led them safely through treacherous waters and trails to the Pacific.

Today, North Dakota's population stands at 660,000, with most residents living in the east. The railroads helped settle North Dakota and promoted its growth. The Northern Pacific utilized ten million acres, one-fourth of the entire state. Nearly half the population in 1890 was foreign born, as the railroads had agents in Europe and in the East, promoting North Dakota to potential emigrants. Most came from Sweden, Norway, Germany, and Russia. These farmers settled in the fertile Red River Valley, and North Dakota became famous for its durham wheat crops.

The Missouri River has been tamed with a series of dams, and Garrison Dam, built in the 1950s, created the two-hundred-mile-long Lake Sakakawea, which has a meandering shoreline of sixteen hundred miles around its bays and coves. The spectacular Four Bears Bridge spans the lake at New Town, and fishermen come here for the abundance of game fish, including northern pike, walleye, and salmon.

The High Plains

The western half of North Dakota is on the Missouri Plateau, which consists of rolling uplands, mesas and buttes, and streams. The Badlands were formed by the carving of thousands of small streams into the steep slopes of clay and silt. Iron ore deposits add ochre and red colors to the Badlands. The Little Missouri River runs through them. This deeply gullied terrain, where short grass grows, is perfect for grazing cattle and sheep. The Badlands thus became the ranching center of the state.

Above:
North Dakota's Badlands were formed by wind and water erosion of sandstone, shale, and clay into banded and multi-colored formations.

Right:
Ronn Moccasin, a Native American, is in charge of the trading post at Fort Union, North Dakota, now a reconstructed historical site.

Left:
On the Prairie Winds Ranch near Bismarck, North Dakota, a pristine moment of tranquillity is captured.

Left:
Fort Union, North Dakota, near the Wyoming border, was once the most important trading post on the Missouri River.

Right:
In tribute to America's first conservationist president, the Theodore Roosevelt National Park was established in his honor in the Badlands of North Dakota, where Roosevelt was once a rancher.

Following page:
Cephus Goddard, a
ninety-two-year-old
rancher, lives in a line
cabin with his wife,
Jesse, near Watford
City. Cowboys would
stay in line cabins
while herding cattle
in the open plains.

Above:
Costumed guides
are available to show
General Custer's house
in Fort Abraham
Lincoln, North Dakota.
Here Custer led his
troops into the Battle
of Little Big Horn,
from which he
never returned.

Theodore Roosevelt made his first foray into the West in 1883 to hunt buffalo and other game. He bought a ranch near the cattle town Medora, and fell in love with the land. After he became president of the United States, he instituted a series of national parks, and more than seventy thousand acres of the Badlands were preserved as the Theodore Roosevelt National Park.

The Logging Camp Ranch, run by John and Jennifer Hanson, is a ten-thousand-acre ranch in the Badlands that has been in the family for four generations. John has taken a conservationist's approach to the land, which differs from the policies of earlier generations. He is replenishing and restocking the land with the future in mind.

As we rode on horseback through the magnificent hills and draws at sunset he spoke of his love for the land, and his sense of belonging to this place became richly apparent. If Hanson typifies the new rancher, there is hope for the survival of the land.

The confluence of the Yellowstone River and the Missouri River was the site of the most important trading post on the Missouri River, Fort Union, established in 1829 by John Jacob Astor's American Fur Company. First beaver pelts, then buffalo hides, were traded. The fort was sold to the army in 1867 and dismantled; troops used its materials to build the nearby Fort Buford.

Buffalo soldiers were stationed at Fort Buford, less than a mile from Fort Union. Two famous Indians were associated with Fort Buford—Sitting Bull surrendered here in 1881, and Chief Joseph of the Nez Perce was brought here after being captured trying to flee with his people to Canada.

Now you can visit a faithful reconstruction of the original Fort Union, complete with soldiers and traders. It was here I met Ronn Moccasin, who heads the trading post, selling blankets, lanterns, and other accouterments of the era. Ronn shared with me how he reclaimed his Indian heritage and spirituality after having grown up unaware of his culture. Today he brings a dignity and self-assurance to his role at the fort.

Custer's Last Command

Fort Abraham Lincoln was built on the Missouri River near Bismarck in 1872. Its first commanding officer was General George Armstrong Custer. Custer lived at the fort with his wife Elizabeth. From here in 1874 Custer led his troops to the Black Hills and precipitated the gold rush to that sacred country of the Sioux, whose legal possession of the hills had been established

Left:
A rancher herds
his cattle down a
ravine on the way to
other grazing lands.

by United States treaty. With obvious disregard for the law, miners started pouring in, and by 1876 there were many skirmishes between the Sioux, the army, and the settlers.

Custer and his men of the Seventh Cavalry set out to round up the warriors, led by Sioux chiefs Sitting Bull and Crazy Horse, on May 17, 1876. On June 25 they met at the Little Big Horn River, and Custer's entire command of troops was killed in the ensuing battle.

Fort Lincoln remains open to visitors today. Tours led by costumed guides speaking the English of Custer's era take you through his house. Reenactments of cavalry and infantry groups celebrate Frontier Army Days each June at the fort.

Country Living

Cephus Goddard and his wife Jesse live on a ranch near Watford City. He's ninety years old, and they've been married fifty-three years. The house they live in was used as a line cabin for cowboys in the 1880s. Ceph, a rancher through and through, yearns for the days when "cattle were all over the dad-blamed country. This country's only fit for cattle. The first homesteader should've been hung if he had a plow with him! I wish it were that way again, all cattle and no fences."

He remembers that, in the old days, during winter, people would get together at one another's houses; cowboys played their fiddles, and there was singing and dancing. Someone would stoke the fire, and all would stay the night, going home or to church the following morning. The first thing you would ask a stranger who came to your place was, "When did you eat last?" Hospitality was the law of the land.

Ceph misses many of his friends, who have passed on. He remarks, "The only worthwhile thing a man or woman can leave when they go to greener pastures are pleasant memories. And I've been left a lot of them."

Ceph, although he says he's "too old for anything," performs at Medora's Burning Hills Amphitheater, reciting his poetry—genuine cowboy poetry. He's never written anything down, but does recall some of them. Here are a few lines from his "Dreamin' and a Dozin'": "Been sitting here on a bench, mind gently roamin' in the noonday sun; never had much religion 'cept my love for the land."

And that's what is common to all the disparate people living in North Dakota. Whether farmer or rancher, living on the plains unites one with the land. The harsh climate, with its elemental extremes and wind that can blow ceaselessly for days, engenders a kind of respect for something that can't be tamed. So you learn to live with it, and come to find out there's no place you'd rather be.

Below:
John Hanson tugs at a bale of hay that is the winter feed for his cattle on his ranch near Bowman, North Dakota.

Right:
Hand carving a paddle at the Trappers and Traders Exhibition at the State Fair in Minot, North Dakota, takes skill and patience.

Right:
At Jamestown,
North Dakota,
a re-created stage
coach robbery
takes place in the
Frontier Village.

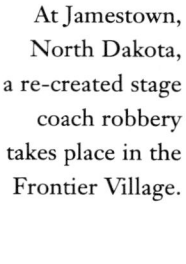

Right:
The farm equip-
ment exhibition
at the State Fair
in Minot, North
Dakota, is domi-
nated by a large,
inflatable tractor.

Left:
Two old North
Dakota natives,
a cowboy and an
Indian, get together
for some friendly
conversation at
the Knife River
Indian Festival.

EPILOGUE

While photographing in the Badlands of South Dakota during winter I climbed a precipice of jagged rocks, looking for unusual angles or vistas to describe the Badlands. I slipped on the crumbling rock and headed toward the edge of the precipice that led to a sharp drop some thirty or forty feet below. I was so engrossed in exploring these unusually eroded formations, which seemed to be from some mysterious world of the past, that I'd forgotten I was alone, with no one to help if need be.

I liked being alone, enjoying the solitude that intensified my discovery of the Badlands. Yet here I was, a few inches from the edge of a cliff and with all my camera gear weighing me down—beauty and danger, side by side.

That is the essence of this country. We look for the beautiful, the benign nature that we feel safe in, but the raw, wild, unpredictable part of nature, complete with danger, is what we get. And somehow that adds to the beauty and uniqueness of the plains. The thin line between beauty and terror, the awareness of being responsible for your own well-being, of knowing how to survive day in and day out among all that this volatile environment offers, is what makes a prairie person.

There is a very strong sense of community in these states. People know their neighbors, help each other out, open their doors to outsiders, and generally believe in treating others as they wish to be treated. They all share common experiences in living on this land, and they recognize that in one another.

I find a great satisfaction in going to the local cafes in towns that I travel through, where farmers in bill caps proclaiming DeKalb or Pioneer Seed or other farm products sit together in groups, drinking coffee, shooting the breeze; Bics clicking in an atmosphere where cigarette smoking is still in favor, talking about the weather and other topics in a laconic shorthand that leaves a tourist unable to read between the lines.

The food is good, too. Homefries, grits, pancakes, biscuits and gravy are my staples as I travel the plains and prairies. Later on in the day, I'll stop at another cafe for homemade pie—coconut custard, banana cream, lemon meringue—all baked from scratch by a woman in town. This cafe society nourishes me—main-street life in a small rural town. If I want to join in a conversation, I am welcome; if I don't, that's all right, too. It's a free country.

Left:
Sunflower and wild-flower wreaths and arrangements are designed at Pipe-stem Creek, near Jamestown, North Dakota, and marketed from here throughout the country.

Right:
A brilliant sunset closes another day where the west begins, silhouetting a windmill driven by the eternal prairie winds.

INDEX